All About
Bats

Project Editors Caryn Jenner, Arpita Nath
Art Editors Emma Hobson, Roohi Rais
Jacket Editor Francesca Young
Jacket Designer Amy Keast
DTP Designers Syed Md Farhan, Dheeraj Singh
Picture Researcher Sumedha Chopra
Producer, Pre-production Nadine King
Producer Srijana Gurung
Managing Editors Soma B. Chowdhury, Laura Gilbert
Managing Art Editors Neha Ahuja Chowdhry, Diane Peyton Jones
Art Director Martin Wilson
Publisher Sarah Larter

Reading Consultant
Jacqueline Harris

Subject Consultant
Dr. Rob Houston

First published in Great Britain in 2017
by Dorling Kindersley Limited
80 Strand, London, WC2R 0RL

Copyright © 2017 Dorling Kindersley Limited
DK, a Penguin Random House Company
16 17 18 19 10 9 8 7 6 5 4 3 2 1
001—298626—January/17

A CIP catalogue record for this book is available from the British Library.

ISBN: 978-0-2412-8263-2

Printed and bound in China.

The publisher would also like to thank the following
for their kind permission to reproduce their photographs:
(Key: a=above, b=below/bottom, c=center, l=left, r=right, t=top)
3 **Dorling Kindersley:** Jerry Young (br). **4–5 123RF.com:** panda3800. **7 Dreamstime.com:** Andrew Burgess
(b). **8–9 Dorling Kindersley:** Rollin Verlinde. **10 Dorling Kindersley:** Jerry Young. **12 Getty Images:**
Christian Heinrich. **13 123RF.com:** shopartgallerycom (cb). **14 123RF.com:** snike (Background).
14–15 Getty Images: Christian Ziegler / Minden Pictures (b). **16–17 Dreamstime.com:** Barbro Bergfeldt
(Background). **18 Dorling Kindersley:** Rollin Verlinde (bl). **19 123RF.com:** Satit Srihin.
22 123RF.com: shop
Jacket images: Fron

Contents

Bats Fly

The sun sets.
It is night time.
Bats fly through the sky!

wing

Bat Wings

There are many
kinds of bats.
They all have
webbed wings
and furry bodies.

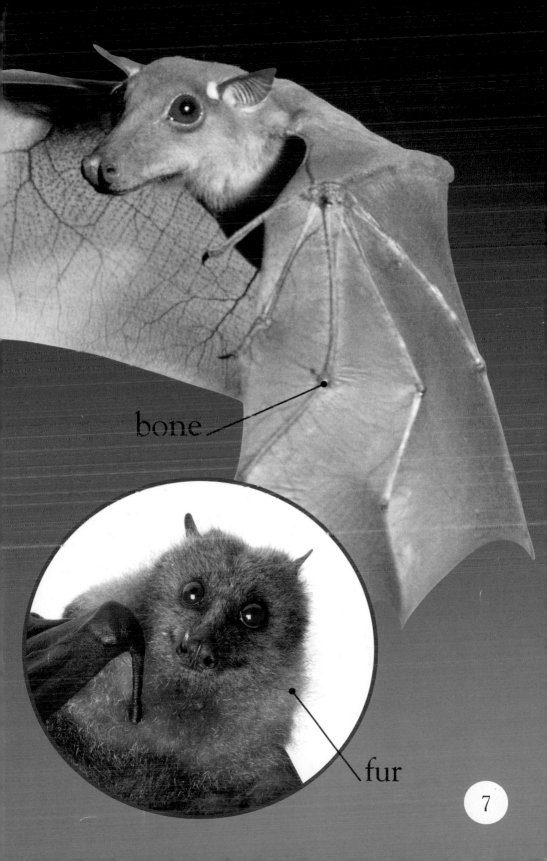

bone

fur

In the Dark

Bats squeak!
They use this sound
to find their way
in the dark.

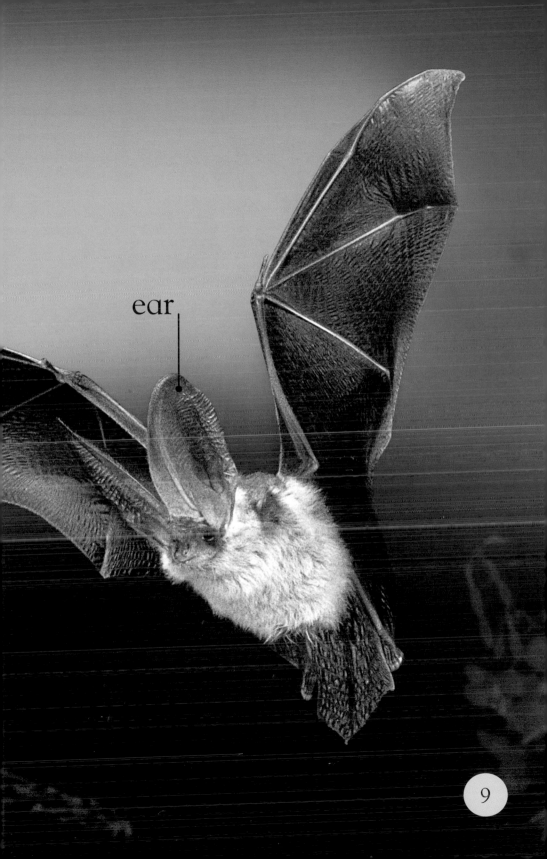

ear

Upside Down

Bats can hang
upside down.
They hold on
with their claws.

claw

teeth

eye

11

Baby Bats

Baby bats are called pups.
This bat mother wraps
her wings around her pup.

bat pup

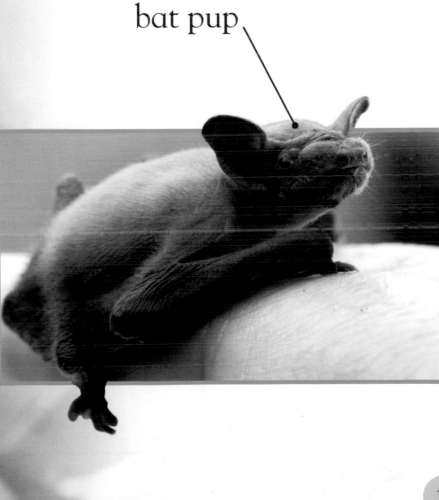

Food for Bats

At night, bats fly about.
They look for food.
Bats eat fruit or
catch insects.

insect

Flying Home

In the morning,
the bats fly home
to sleep.

Homes for Bats

Some bats find homes
in old buildings.
Some bats live
high up in trees.

Bat Cave

These bats live together
in a big bat cave.
Shh! They are sleeping.

Glossary

Bat pup
baby bat

Claw
sharp nails used to
hold, climb and grab

Insect
type of small animal
that crawls or flies

Webbed
fingers or toes joined
with a piece of skin

Wing
part of body used by
some animals for flying

Index

A Note to Parents

DK Readers is a four-level interactive reading adventure series for children, developing the habit of reading widely for both pleasure and information.

Beautiful illustrations and superb full-colour photographs combine with engaging, easy-to-read narratives to offer a fresh approach to each subject in the series. Each DK Reader is guaranteed to capture a child's interest while developing his or her reading skills, general knowledge, and love of reading.

The four levels of DK Readers are aimed at different reading abilities, enabling you to choose the books that are exactly right for your child:

Level 1: Learning to read
Level 2: Beginning to read
Level 3: Beginning to read alone
Level 4: Reading alone

The "normal" age at which a child begins to read can be anywhere from three to eight years old. Adult participation through the lower levels is very helpful for providing encouragement, discussing storylines, and sounding out unfamiliar words.

No matter which level you select, you can be sure that you are helping your child learn to read, then read to learn!